John de Satgé

Letters to an Ordinand
A STUDY IN VOCATION

Published in conjunction with
the Advisory Council for the Church's Ministry

London SPCK

First published 1976
SPCK
Holy Trinity Church
Marylebone Road
London NW1 4DU

Printed in Great Britain by
Bocardo and Church Army Press, Cowley, Oxford.

ISBN 0 281 02948 2

For

JEREMY AND NICHOLAS
who sometimes ask such questions

CONTENTS

FOREWORD BY THE
BISHOP OF ST EDMUNDSBURY AND IPSWICH

John de Satgé has been involved in the selection and training of men for the ministry for many years. He has written
this book out of close knowledge of the questions that face
any man who is trying to decide whether God is calling him
to be a parson in the Church of England, or whether his
idea of offering himself for work is a passing fantasy. Often
it isn't at all easy to be sure what God's will for us really is.
I think that this book will help men in that position to
think about God's call more clearly and honestly. In most
of Gregory's letters there is a good deal to ponder, and I
am privileged to commend them, not only to prospective
ordinands, but to everyone concerned with the ordained
ministry of the Church.

LESLIE ST EDM. AND IPSWICH
Chairman of the Advisory Council for the Church's Ministry

INTRODUCTION

For nearly ten years I was director of ordinands in a
northern diocese, responsible also for the further training
of junior clergymen. During the same period I served on
many selection boards attended by potential clergy; and
my 'external' work as a residentiary canon involved many
conversations, most of them encouraging but some quite
the reverse, with experienced parish priests. Both before
and since that time I have taught theology to Anglican
ordinands and have discussed their future with them.

All this has sharpened my interest in the mystery of
vocation. Why does one man feel insistently the call of God
to the full-time ministry, while another, apparently better
fitted for it, does not? What of the man whose persistent
sense of call the Church is as persistently unable to recognize? Are there occasions when an able man with the
strongest Christian motivation should be discouraged from
seeking ordination on the grounds that he could make a
greater contribution by remaining a layman? Is the frustration of some experienced clergy attributable to the fact
that they had originally been called inwardly to Christian
service other than in the Ministry, to which they had been
unwisely directed? What are we to make of a self-supporting (non-stipendiary) 'auxiliary pastoral ministry'? Most
important of all, perhaps, is the question which underlies
so many others — how may a man be helped to recognize a
genuine call to the ministry, distinguishing it from the
many other avenues proper to Christian obedience?

The letters in this little book are written as a device to
bring out most of the issues in the 'inward' side of vocation.
They are written by one Gregory to a young man called
Christopher — the symbolism of the names is obvious —
and cease at the point where the latter is about to attend
an ACCM Selection Conference. The opinions expressed in

the letters, some of them no doubt controversial, are essentially my own; but I hope that even where they provoke disagreement they may still prove stimulating to some who are wondering whether ordination may be for them, and also to some who have to advise such people. For more convenient use I have indicated the principal topic in each letter.

1 INTRODUCING THE CORRESPONDENTS

My dear Christopher,

I am delighted to hear that you are thinking of ordination
in the Church of England, but I am not really surprised.
I remember a conversation we had a couple of years back.
Now you are in your second year at the University, it is
obviously a good moment to explore very seriously the
possibilities.

But it is still only a matter of exploring possibilities. You
don't want to get too set on it too soon. There are plenty
of other ways in which a committed Christian can properly
serve his Lord. What is more, a square peg in that particular
round hole can do so much harm; and if later on you find
you have to get out of it, it is bound to involve the most
painful clashes of loyalty. A great Christian stalwart of
fifty years ago, Bishop Taylor Smith, used to say there
were two things a man should not undertake without the
strongest inner compulsion: marriage and ordination. He
remained a bachelor!

Fortunately there are plenty of people to advise you
and to make as sure as anyone can that you have the right
motivation. You probably know that there are two author-
ities involved in selecting and training candidates for the
ministry, the bishop of the diocese where you live and the
Advisory Council for the Church's Ministry which operates
from Church House, Westminster, to co-ordinate standards
between the many dioceses; so you get a double check.
Church people are often critical of ACCM, as the central
body is known for short, but my impression is that it does
a lot to make our Church's selection procedures as good as
they are and that they will at least stand comparison with
their equivalents in any other profession. I hope that you
are already in touch with your diocese. In most cases the

1

bishop works through a priest whom he has appointed to be Director of Ordinands; your own parish priest will no doubt be able to put you in touch.

Meanwhile I shall of course be happy to help where I can. If, for example, you liked to write to me from time to time, I could give a running commentary on the way you are looking at things. I don't think that it is up to me to do much in the way of suggesting things. I see my brief as essentially a watching one. A little reflection, and perhaps research, will show you that that is why I shall sign myself in these letters

> Your devoted friend,
> *Gregory*

2 RECOGNIZING A 'SENSE OF VOCATION'

My dear Christopher,

Yes, it is difficult to know what a 'sense of vocation' should be like. A 'call' has to be mediated through all the complexities of a human personality, and no two people are quite alike. That is why it is so risky to compare your own experience with someone else's. Occasionally you will hear another man's story which throws light on your own case; but that light can deceive you, if you start trying to cram your own experience into the other man's mould. To read about other people can help, but be sure that you look at several very different case-histories.

One factor which recurs in many people's awareness of being called to the ministry is the sense of being 'nudged'. All sorts of different things seem to conspire together to make you look in that direction. It might start from admiration for some priest — or by irritation with him leading you to wonder whether you might not do it better yourself! The 'Why not me?' thought may seem negative, but it is at least a beginning. I suppose, however, most committed church people have the odd moment of wondering about it; it is not until the idea gets to be persistent or recurring that you should take it seriously. The element of accumulation is important. It is when all manner of things, mostly trivial in themselves, suggest the beginnings of a pattern that you become aware of being 'nudged' in a certain direction.

But do remember that the ministry is not the only occupation to which a man can feel himself being insistently directed. Indeed I am sure that far too many committed, idealistic Christian men have assumed too readily that God wanted them in the ordained ministry and so have hardly glanced at the other opportunities open to them.

So don't go too far along that road, even in your own private thoughts, without doing some checking. There are two basic co-ordinates to watch for: the ministry is concerned with other people for the sake of God and with God for the sake of other people; and (in the direction where you are looking) it is ministry within the Church of England as that Church understands it and provides opportunities for it.

It is astonishing how often that last point, so obvious, gets overlooked. If you don't really know what a clergyman does with his time, for goodness sake find out before you go any further. The vast majority of clergymen work in parishes, but within the parochial ministry there are many different patterns of work. There are also, of course, a variety of chaplaincies and other specialized jobs. If you cannot honestly see yourself at home in any of them, think again about the whole venture; perhaps even look at the ministry as it is worked out in other Christian bodies.

A special caution about 'reforming'. One has met ordinands and clergy who are full of zeal to reform the Church because they feel its structures are too tied to the past to be useful today. That is all to the good. But there comes a point beyond which the Church to which the critic feels himself to be committed has ceased to be the Church in which he works; his zeal, and perhaps his frustrations, have led him into a fantasy world. He is not likely to find fulfilment in his ministry; and from the parishioner's point of view, it is not helpful to have Don Quixote for your vicar.

Yours ever,
Gregory

3 SOCIAL WORK, COMMUNICATION, AND PRIESTHOOD

My dear Christopher,

I am very happy to enlarge on what I wrote last time about the 'first co-ordinate' of ministry: 'Ministry is concerned with other people for the sake of God and with God for the sake of other people'. We must make some big distinctions. Of course it is perfectly proper to be concerned with other people for their own sake, and one rejoices that so many Christians are. Present day life affords many opportunities for following out fully humanitarian concerns. But the ministry of the Church is not one of them. Those who enter it with that motivation are all too likely to end up in the hopeless frustration that I described in my last letter.

The other extreme, concern with God without much involvement with other people, is much more rare in our 'practically' orientated society. But there have been people in the past, and there probably still are some, whose concern with God has caused them to withdraw from human contacts: contemplatives, we might call them, holy men, mystics, hermits, members of the enclosed religious orders. They are often the true 'theologians' — those who know God for himself — and it is wrong to write them off as anti-social. Was it not St Antony, the greatest of the hermits, who said 'My life and my death are in my neighbour'? Their withdrawal is the road along which they follow their particular call from the same God who summons others to full humanitarian service. If, therefore, your inner life honestly pursued leads you to a devotion to God where your fellow human beings come as an unwelcome intrusion, it may be that God is calling you to something different from the Church of England ministry.

Turning to the positive side, I would say that the person

concerned with other people for the sake of God and with God for the sake of other people is marked above all by 'the pastoral heart'. Most ordained ministers find that their gifts and inclinations approximate either to those of the social worker or to those of the professional communicator. A priest is at a disadvantage without some measure of the gifts needed in both those professions; but they are not essential for him as the pastoral heart undoubtedly is.

The priest with the social worker slant will be concerned with people in the actual situation of their lives. He may well find himself deeply involved in local community affairs. He will need to watch, lest his commitments there make him neglect the more 'churchy' side of his work.

The priest in whom the communicator's drives are uppermost will long for people to share his delight in the faith. He will spend as long as he can wrestling with that faith so as to express most intelligibly its true proportions. His temptation is to be so concerned for Christian truth that he has no time (literally as well as metaphorically) for those who do not appreciate it. His ministry is not, after all, only to the receptive.

In a word: the urge to help people in their social conditions and the desire to communicate the Christian faith adequately are both valid Christian concerns. The Christian minister needs to have something of them both. But if either of them becomes his overriding concern, he might for his own satisfaction and for his greatest contribution to the cause be better placed as a layman.

Yours as ever,
Gregory

4 THE PASTORAL HEART

My dear Christopher,

Oh dear — but I suppose I asked for it! How does one write about the pastoral heart without being mawkish? It's easy enough to spot the quality when you meet it — and unfortunately to detect its absence at some critical moment. Just run over in your mind the features you most appreciate in the clergy you know; most of them will be the products of a pastoral heart. Still, you asked me for what I think it is, so here goes.

The man with a pastoral heart has time for you when you need him; even if he is run off his feet he will spare you a moment to fix an appointment. And when you actually talk with him you will have the impression that he is listening to you with interest. In other words he has a courtesy which is nothing to do with his degree of social polish. You will find it easy to talk to him even if he is as shy as you are.

Because he is concerned about people he will himself be vulnerable. Yet he will be without self-pity and will be adept at coping with disappointment. He will be perceptive enough to see triumphs in what other people might interpret as modified disaster when weak or stupid people choose the lesser evil. He will have the self-control to suspend his own feelings (though if he is unaware of them or suppresses them he won't last long) so as to weep with those who weep and rejoice with those who rejoice. He will be cast down when people fail to respond to what moves him so deeply, but equally he will be elated when he comes across a shaft of unexpected generosity lighting an unpromising human situation. He will be capable of great anger in face of physical or moral squalor, but his delight in primroses on a dunghill will outweigh his disgust at their setting.

The pastorally hearted man may well have moments of envy but he will not let it cloud his judgement. So, if he is of the 'social worker' type, he will be delighted to find lay professionals helping his people at levels where he himself is powerless to help. If he is more of a 'communicator', he will build with thankfulness on what some professor or publicist earning four times as much as himself has written.

In short, the man with the pastoral heart is content with his lot, though he will not be content with what he has managed to do. That is a paradox which only makes sense in terms of his belief that he is where he is and is doing what he is doing because God wants it that way.

If you turn out to be such a man, you may not have much or be much in the eyes of the world, but you will have a happiness beyond any other than I could wish you.

Yours as ever,
Gregory

5 STAYING POWER AND SPIRITUAL DISCIPLINE

My dear Christopher,

Of course you are right when you say that a man's pastoral heart is sustained by his inner spiritual resources. Such a person is almost sure to be a man who lives by some regular routine; though there may be almost as many routines as there are people concerned.

A generation ago one would have not said that. There were then two main routines — and those variants of one — which clergymen normally followed. The Middle and High churchmen had as an ideal the morning pattern of Mattins, a period for silent meditation, and, when the parish programme allowed it, Holy Communion. At the other end of the day Evensong probably divided the afternoon activities from the evening's. All those services were held in the church building, and the 'offices' were recited aloud even if no congregation was present. The solitary priest saying both sides in the responsory prayers did so as the representative of the people committed to his care. He would probably spend time after the set prayers interceding silently and systematically, street by street, for his parishioners and their needs; it was as much a part of his pastoral responsibility as of his personal discipline of prayer. Late at night in the privacy of his own room he would make his more personal prayers.

The Evangelical parson followed much the same routine, though he was more likely to vary the Prayer Book services by something less formal; and he was less likely to say his prayers either in an empty church or to have so many weekday services of Holy Communion. His general emphasis would be less sacramental and more dependent upon receiving the Word of God by meditating on the Scriptures. The practice of family prayers persisted (and still persists) more frequently in Evangelical than in other clerical households.

The ideals were fine and their fruits in spiritual stability often rich and abundant, but the blessing could become a burden. It was perhaps best suited to those clergy who staffed parishes where there were several curates, especially if they lived in a clergy-house, for the routine was one adapted from a college or cathedral model. The strain to the man on his own could be crippling, especially if his rule of life did not include the relief that comes from regular sacramental confession.

My impression is that the old uniformity of ideal, if not of practice, has gone. Liturgical changes have ended the old uniformity of the Book of Common Prayer and changing times have shown the need for a more flexible attitude. On balance I believe the gains have exceeded the losses. The spiritual strength needed by today's ministers must be adaptable as well as tough. But against that, one should take account of the power which comes from accepting a binding obligation to fulfil a discipline except when it is strictly impossible.

Surely the essential is to find some way of building into a busy life a regular space in which to be quiet, to be deliberately open to God for receiving confirmation in calling, a deepening acquaintance with him, and a renewed experience of his grace in forgiveness and acceptance. Without such a space there is a serious risk that an over-busy and conscientious man will be without spiritual income, living on dwindling capital and forced back on his own resources instead of on God's. Finally, it is so desirable as to be almost essential that there should be the closest link between the minister's personal spirituality and the forms of worship in which he gives a public lead.

> Yours ever,
> *Gregory*

6 PRIEST AND PEOPLE AT PRAYER

My dear Christopher,

My apologies; I agree that the final sentence of my last letter was so compressed as to let in little if any light.

My point was the need to connect a priest's personal religion with his professional activities in public worship. The old practice of saying Morning and Evening Prayer daily helped to form the minister's own spirituality in the mould of 'common prayer', that is, the prayer which all church people shared. Its influence extended far: for example, the workman hearing the bell for Evensong might bow his head for a moment as the parson knelt in church. Vague, you may think, tenuous, meaning progressively less and less as society moves away from the village model presupposed by the old Prayer Book; yet still a reminder. Even now, the sight of a church or the sound of its bell, even the spectacle of a parson, are useful reminders to a secular society of the divine in its midst.

The great danger in thinking about the Christian ministry as intensively as we are in these letters is of considering the minister himself in splendid isolation; the widespread and deplorable habit of calling ordination 'going into the Church' is a symptom. A priest unconnected with other people is in as unnatural a situation as Robinson Crusoe on his island. Even when he is quite detached from parochial responsibility, a priest remains part and parcel of the Church understood as the People of God.

Ironically it can happen that a priest is more isolated in a parish situation than in any other. That is sometimes because the laity feel the priest is there to 'do it all for them'. Or it can happen that a priest resents supposed encroachments on his proper preserves. There has been a great deal of talk in recent years about 'the mission of the whole

Church', about 'the witness of the laity', about the clergy as 'enablers', whose function is to make the ordinary Christian more effective in his normal spheres of work and leisure. All of this should have brought the relation between clergy and laity into better focus. In many cases it has.

But in others it has not. An enthusiastic layman, for example, starts some excellent new activity within and beyond the circle of the faithful, and then moves away to another district, leaving yet another organization for the vicar to run. Or a group of deeply committed youngsters get across a conservatively-minded churchwarden, who for years has done the lion's share of keeping the church plant going but who is deeply scandalized by the use of pop music in church; the depth of commitment on both sides is beyond question.

Such people may be at loggerheads, but they are still bound together in Christian relationships, and the priest is involved with them all. The one choice he cannot make is to opt out. He has himself to bear the animosity, and to do so he will need all the resources open to him. His own point of crisis may well be reached in the church building, in the strain of leading people whom he knows to be out of love and charity, in united worship.

Even without such complications the fact of having to 'lead' other people in worship at the same time as you yourself are trying to worship can be a strain. It takes discipline and preparation; it demands a basic appreciation of worship as a worthwhile activity. If you don't like church worship, it could be an indication that ordination is not really for you. So you see how important it is that the priest's personal devotion underpins his conduct of public worship. Every priest must work out for himself the exact relationship between the two.

Yours ever,
Gregory

7 THE BASIC SECURITIES OF FAITH

My dear Christopher,

I think you have made a fair point when you say that the spiritual resources I described in my last letter are all matters which the minister 'does': conducting public worship, saying the Church's offices, etc. The resources, you say, come from the man's own discipline, not from the bounty of God. Yes — but also, Yes and no. The distinction is less sharp than you suggest. The man's faithfulness in sticking to his offices can come from his experience of God's grace; and through his obedience, and his failures in obedience, God's grace can reach him at deeper levels of his being. The ways of God are more complex than you might suppose.

Nevertheless you have a point, and it gains strength from the way you connect it with the recurring problem of anyone who tries to be sensitive to God's will. How can I be sure that it really is God's will for me to move in a given direction? I suggest that while total certainty in this present life is a will-o'-the-wisp — as St Paul put it, we walk by faith not by sight — there are certain indications which give us at least grounds for a working hypothesis. I mention three whose presence has stood many people besides myself in good stead. They do not necessarily occur in the order in which I am going to describe them. I will try to express them as basically as possible, in language which you might call 'neutral'. You can translate them into whatever theological idiom you find most acceptable.

First, there is the haunting sense of being caught up into something that is already going on; something huge; something which eventually will make sense of all experience. Call it the divine purpose in the world. Despite all evidences to the contrary, it is there, happening long before we existed, happening long after we are dead. We are caught up into it, we have a share however minute; and, greatly daring, we want to co-operate. In your present enquiries you are trying to discover your own appointed niche.

The corollary to that is that you have to come to terms with your own failure: your divided mind, your preference for the comfortable second-best, whatever it may be. You are beginning to learn what it means to be ashamed in the presence of God and not to run away. You are learning the surprising fact that God accepts you, even though he does not necessarily approve of you. This is a fundamental fact of Christian existence which some people come to grips with through sacramental confession, and others realize by 'feeding on the promises of God', after the manner of the Comfortable Words in the 1662 Book of Common Prayer. If you are to go forward as a serious candidate for Holy Orders, the certainty of divine forgiveness must, by one means or another, be built into your inmost experience.

A third condition is harder to analyse. It is the awareness of God in action, the living God, the Holy Spirit: in you and in other people, between you and other people, binding you together so that you share in the purpose and the mercy of God with each other; a growing awareness of the Church as fellowship, of other people completing your incompleteness and you completing theirs. John Donne's famous words spring to mind: "No man is an island . . .".

I hope these three matters ring a bell, however faint, in your experience. They are, of course, theological in the deepest sense, involving the central doctrines of the Christian faith. But you don't need to appreciate the theology for the power it describes to operate in your life. That power is the one and only thing completely necessary to make all this talk about vocation and ministry worthwhile. To be quite honest, if it rings no bell, you had better forget about the whole thing until it does.

Your candid friend,
Gregory

14

8 CONCERNING THE BIBLE

My dear Christopher,

Are you a regular reader of the Bible? Something you said in answering my last letter made me wonder if you had learned to take full advantage of what the Bible read intelligently can do for your inner devotion. You do not need to hold Fundamentalist views about the Bible to find in it the nourishment which your spirit needs. That is the immediate importance. A longer-term point is that, if you do go forward to the formal study of theology, you will have to study the Bible historically. That will land you with books without number *about* the Bible, books which assume a basic knowledge of what is actually *in* the Bible. If you have not that basic knowledge, you will be at a disadvantage.

Don't waste too much time sorting out just why the Bible in all its diversity should hold the importance it does for twentieth-century faith; you are unlikely to find any really convincing answer. Accept instead the simple fact that all through the Christian centuries your co-religionists of every variety have found that, in reading and pondering the Bible, they have come to know God better, to the strengthening of their faith and character. You have been admitted into a long tradition. Don't try to understand it in advance; practise it and in the practice you may find some clues towards understanding it.

I hope, too, that your Bible reading follows some regular system. We are fortunate nowadays in the amount of help readily at hand; no need for feats of brute endurance like starting in at Genesis One and reading a chapter a day straight through! It may help to follow one of the 'schemes' which give you a passage of the Bible each day to read with explanatory comments: the Bible Reading Fellowship or, if you prefer something more definitely Evangelical, the Scripture Union, both have good schemes. If there is a Bible Study group at your Church, so much the better; but go to it as well as persevering with your own daily reading, not as a substitute for it. Don't despise the value of a good habit!

It is frequently good to read a passage in more than one translation, and money spent in equipping yourself with a battery of half-a-dozen versions will not be wasted. Personally I find the Revised Standard Version (now officially recommended to Roman Catholics in the edition 'The Common Bible') the best general-purpose English text, with the Jerusalem Bible and the New English Bible my favourites for comparison.

An aspect of Bible reading worth remembering is to use the Epistle and Gospel for the following Sunday (and, of course, the Old Testament reading if your church has one). It has the advantage of bringing together your Bible reading and your sacramental life as a regular communicant. Mulling over the passages week by week may lead you to want your own commentary. That takes us well outside the scope of these letters, but it is worth stressing the need for taking reliable advice before buying Bible commentaries. There are so many on the market and they vary so much that it is easy to lash out a lot of money unwisely.

But one way or another, do build reflective reading of the Bible firmly into your devotional programme. You will often find that such reading leads directly into prayer; but even when it does not it will often add to your grasp of the faith and of the God who is the centre and the point of the whole exercise.

Yours as always,
Gregory

16

My dear Christopher,

I am sure that you are right to connect the fashion current among some clergymen to belittle sermons with a lack of confidence in the Bible and its authority. It is an unsatisfactory business, not least because it makes for a climate of opinion where preachers expect to give and congregations to receive little.

In fact, it can be a sign of more than one thing. If it refers to the changed means of communication nowadays — looking more than listening, discussion rather than monologue, etc. — then it can be a help in reminding the preacher to keep fresh in his techniques. But criticism of the sermon as a means of communication sometimes masks a disbelief in the authoritative aspects of the Christian faith, the ancient declaration, 'Thus saith the Lord.' If so, it should be seen as a failure of nerve and resisted.

Since the moment of its independence from the medieval Roman Church, the Church of England has gloried in the true catholicism of the Word, and has insisted that its ministers be above all ministers of that Word. In the reformed ordination service of the Prayer Book the priest-candidate is handed a Bible at the moment when he receives symbolically the tools of his trade; in the older service it was a chalice. The change implies no disrespect to the sacraments; rather it honours them by showing their true place as the means by which the faithful receive the living Word.

The difficulties in getting across the Christian message today need to be taken most seriously. They should not make us give up the attempt, but encourage us to ask far-reaching questions about what it is we are really trying to do. Why, for example, is the sermon normally given in the context of a service? Does that mean it is something essentially different from, say, a lecture? Are the scripture readings in a service to be considered together with the sermon as forming part of 'the ministry of the Word'? What is the connection between preaching and discussion groups and less formal gatherings for mutual enlightenment? How far can the Christian message be communicated through quite other media, drama, music, the visual arts? What about 'non-verbal communication'? Can people learn the faith or deepen their experience of it by sharing in activity projects?

These and a dozen other questions may lead you to revise your estimate of preaching, and of the function of the sermon in the preaching task. They may well explode the conventional notion of preaching as one man spouting and the others listening or dozing. You will probably find yourself looking at preaching as a corporate activity in which the congregation (not at all the same thing as an audience) has a part to play, an activity which doesn't start when the preacher enters the pulpit or finish when he leaves it. Actions, it is often said, speak louder than words, but actions are often ambiguous and their subtlety lost without the word of interpretation.

Yours ever,
Gregory

10 CONCERNING 'CHURCHINESS'

My dear Christopher,

I think I know what you mean by 'churchiness', though it is hard to be precise. The word is always used in a bad sense, and the phenomena it describes are mostly very un-attractive. However, it is easy to be a bit too sweeping in one's criticisms and indeed one can walk dangerously near to the edge of arrogance and hypocrisy.

Those who feel that church life is important must take proper responsibility for its arrangements. 'Let all things be done decently and in order', insisted St Paul; and there is a wide margin where what is seemly to one person is fussy to another; rather like the varying degrees of house- and garden-pride.

'Churchiness' descends from a foible to a vice when the horizon of a person's concern stretches no further than the church buildings and what happens inside them; or when social and political judgements are made on the basis of church advantage to the exclusion of the wider community. Here again, however, one needs to guard against premature judgement. Support for a church view on some moral sub-ject may reflect the conviction that it is of benefit to the entire community, not just the minority of churchgoers. Perhaps the hardest to cope with is that rather pathetic kind of person who finds in the church and the minutiae of its arrangements a sense of purpose, of being valued and of belonging. That person's 'churchiness' may well be the only bridge leading out of isolation.

Perhaps you had in mind the prevalence of clerical 'shop'. Of course, any group of persons sharing professional interests, skills, and concerns will have their own particular topics of conversation. Any specialized jargon will seem strange to someone outside the group, but clerical shop

19

can be particularly bizarre and off-putting to a sensitive layman, because of the matter-of-fact way in which it deals with sacred subjects. Clergymen do face a real danger of allowing their familiarity with holy things to degenerate into flippancy; but the layman must remember that what to him may be kept in a special compartment for rare use is to the clergyman the regular stuff of his business. There may well be errors of taste or misjudgement of occasion; but many of the trappings of religion are better not taken too solemnly.

An altogether more serious matter is the different way of looking at things which a parson often has from a layman. In part it is a matter of being instructed in theology: much clergyman's talk about 'the Church' involves a range of deeply religious associations: a spiritual society, the Body of Christ, the People of God. Where many laymen will see a collection of individuals, some of whom he knows socially and some of whom he does not, who happen to like attending a certain type of service, the parson will see an example, however imperfect, of the Holy Spirit transforming individuals into a fellowship, a sacramental and supernatural thing. If laymen would learn a little theology and clergymen would translate their jargon without watering down its content, many misunderstandings would not appear. One of the more hopeful signs of the present time is the number of laymen — teachers, for example, but others too — who are studying theology outside a clerical context. I am sure that some of the more offensive 'churchiness' would be dispelled by the ending of the parson's theological monopoly.

I am glad that you raised this prickly matter. Try to understand professional 'churchiness' and to distinguish between the harmless and the nasty. But if you really find the whole thing repellent, it is perhaps a small pointer against your being ordained.

As ever,
Gregory

11 'WHAT EXACTLY IS A PRIEST?'

My dear Christopher,

'What exactly is a priest?' you ask. I find that question
the more interesting because it is so seldom asked. People
ask a good deal about what a priest does or should do or
does not do, but very little about what he is. You say that
in my letter about 'churchiness' I talked about a clerical
'caste', using apparently indiscriminately the words
'parson', and 'clergyman'; while in earlier letters I had
spoken about 'the priest.' Are they all names for the same
thing, you wonder; and what about 'minister'? Are they
the same sort of thing as their counterparts in the Free
Churches and the Roman Catholic Church?

It would be interesting to put these questions to a
number of Anglican clergymen and compare their answers.
They would, no doubt, give very different ones, but I
suspect that you could arrange them broadly into two
groups. There would be those who believed that their
ordination by a bishop had placed them in a particular and
permanent 'order' within the general run of church people.
Whatever form their work might take, whatever their
future, even if it involved disaster or disgrace, they would
belong for ever to the order of priesthood. Their ordination
had given them a 'sacramental character', which nothing,
not even death, could remove. They would insist that that
was true of all who had been ordained properly ('validly')
by a bishop standing in the true succession, Anglican,
Roman Catholic, or Eastern Orthodox. They would not
make the same claims for a minister appointed other than
by episcopal ordination; their opinions of the status of
such ministers would probably vary. They would hasten to
add that the high claims they made for their office had
nothing to do with their own personal goodness, that in

fact, it carried awesome responsibilities. But that was the way in which God worked.

The second main group of Anglican priests would find such notions strange to them and perhaps offensive. Negatively, they would feel that the only genuine 'sacramental character' came from their status given at baptism, and so at the deepest level they were no different from any other baptized member of the Church. What ordination had done was to set them aside, with the highest possible credentials, for certain tasks within the Church. They were thus authorized or 'accredited' to perform those functions in the name of the Lord, and they were assured of his power as well as his authority in doing them. But, they would insist, though it was no ordinary Christian job that they were set aside to do, in themselves they remained ordinary Christian men.

I am glad that you have raised this question. Many people would consider it academic in the bad sense, unimportant. Indeed, in the old days when the parson was a recognized and accepted (if often ignored) figure in the local scene, you could get along perfectly well without bothering about any such 'theoretical' questions, but now it is different. The clergyman's role no longer goes unchallenged in the technological world. It is important for him to be clear about what he is. He has enough to worry him, without being crippled by a permanent crisis of identity.

Both types of view are currently held among the clergy of our Church. You do not have to make an absolute choice between them, of course — both are eminently respectable — and you may well want to defer your own preference until you have made some formal study of theology. But what you can usefully do at this stage is to ask yourself: If God is really calling me to the ordained ministry, what sort of adjustments will I have to be prepared to make in my fundamental relationships with other people, especially with my fellow-Christians who are not so ordained?

Yours ever,
Gregory

12 CONTRADICTION, COMPROMISE, AND COMPREHENSIVENESS

My dear Christopher,

I understand only too well your dismay at the conflicting estimates of their priesthood which different Anglican clergymen hold. But that is how it is, and if you are considering joining their ranks, you must accept it. It is a part of what is meant when people speak of the 'comprehensiveness' of the Church of England and the wider Anglican Communion of which it forms a part. Some people consider it a strength, others a weakness; and while one should not exaggerate the differences, it is plain dishonest to pretend that they are not there.

There are three main ways of handling this comprehensiveness. 1. You can decide that of any two conflicting views, one is right and the other to be rejected. 2. You can try to combine them into a synthesis. 3. You can hold them both together in uneasy tension, postponing choice or synthesis until other factors have appeared to make the position clearer. Each of these methods is appropriate at some point and inappropriate at others. Unless you are to sit ineffectually on the fence, you will often have to choose in such a way as to say, 'That is where I stand'. But if it is in conscience at all possible, you should go on to add, 'So far as I can see the alternative is false, but other people, from where they stand, may well see it differently'. In other words, it is often possible to hold a position provisionally as well as firmly, and thus avoid the final breach of discrediting those who differ from you. Only by an attitude which is basically inclusive rather than exclusive can the unity of Anglicanism be maintained.

All this came out of the conflicting views about the ministry held among Anglicans. To my mind that matter is clearly one for postponing judgement. The appeal to history does not help much, nor do the official documents of the Church, for different interpretations are possible. If modern revisions of church services and Canon, that is, church, Law tend to favour the first view that I outlined, the 'sacramental', more 'Catholic' one, their older counterparts are far less clear. Ordination has certainly consistently been held to set a man aside from his fellow-Christians, but the Order to which the priest was admitted is described in terms at least as legal in flavour as theological. The ordained minister had his proper place in the hierarchical society of Tudor England, only the palest ghost of which still walks the land today. It is curiously hard to find what anyone today would call a coherent 'theology of the ministry' in the writings of those who shaped Elizabeth I's church settlement; those were not the terms in which people thought. This letter is no place for pursuing historical enquiry further. All we can say is that the appeal to history does not decide unequivocally between the rival views of the Ministry.

Can you then synthesize these views? Theologians are currently conducting background studies which may prove helpful, digging behind the formularies and interpretations to uncover whatever basic notions may be held in common. What is more, this work is being done by teams of theologians co-operating right across the denominational barriers. But it will take time. The failure a few years ago of the proposals for Anglican-Methodist unity to convince many responsible people at both ends of the Anglican spectrum (to say nothing of the Methodists) stands as a warning against premature synthesis.

For the present we must accept co-existence with all its difficulties. Personally I see that as a challenge, a source of hope, but however you look at it, it remains a fact.

Ever yours,
Gregory

13 THE PROFESSIONAL CHARACTER
OF PRIESTHOOD

My dear Christopher,

I am grateful to you for pointing out that the term
'character' has other senses than that in Catholic sacramental theology. There is, as you say, the sense of 'professional'
character. A priest's professional character should mean
that you know where you are when you go to see him; just
as with a doctor or a solicitor, there are certain attitudes
and relationships which you can rightly expect.

Not everyone would agree. Some would deny that a
priest is, or ought to be, a professional in any sense
analogous to that of an accountant, for example. They would
point to the harm done by the stereotyped parson so
fatuously, or so odiously, caricatured by many a comedian.
The second objection applies of course as much to most
professions; think of the many wicked solicitors of fiction!

The first objection is more serious. I agree that the
ministry is a profession only with a difference but so, in the
end, is any other. Professor G. R. Dunstan discussed the
matter most helpfully in a contribution to the booklet
which he edited under the title *The Sacred Ministry* (SPCK
1970). He took up the concept of a profession as defined
by the sociologist R. K. Merton:

> First, the value placed upon systematic knowledge and
> the intellect: knowing. Second, the value placed upon
> technical skill and trained capacity: doing. And third,
> the value placed upon putting this conjoint knowledge
> and skill to work in the service of others: helping. It is
> these three values as fused in the concept of a profes-
> sion that enlist the respect of men.

The professional character of the priest in this sense may
be said to be marked by a systematic knowledge of theology,

the ways of understanding God's presence and activity; a trained capacity to apply that knowledge in human situations; and a determination to place that knowledge and skill at the disposal of others. Such 'knowing, doing, and helping' gives a priest the character which marks his professional attitudes, whatever particular responsibilities he may have. People who meet him professionally have the right to expect of him such a character. It is along those lines that his accountability lies — and accountability is another mark of any profession as we are using the concept.

You may perhaps feel two things about this description. First, it applies to any Christian, whether or not he is episcopally ordained, who functions in a ministerial capacity. I agree. The 'character' under discussion is not the sacramental character of Catholic theology. Ordination seals or authenticates professional character by giving it public authority. It is theoretically as possible to have a man ordained who lacks this character as to have a layman who embodies it without official recognition.

A second point which will not have escaped you is that our discussion of professional character has led us back by a different route to the point reached much earlier in these letters, the supreme importance of 'the pastoral heart'. But you will be able to reflect on that remarkable circumstance without further comment from me.

Yours ever,
Gregory

26

14 CONCERNING NON-STIPENDIARY PRIESTS

My dear Christopher,

The 'professional' understanding of ministerial 'character' does indeed have a bearing on the issue of 'part-time' clergy, though not in the decisive way which you suggest; but first, let us define our terms, for the current discussion is often confused before it starts. It is about priests who are paid for their pastoral work and priests who earn their living in other ways, receiving only their expenses incurred in church work: stipendiary priests, if you like, or non-stipendiary.

Western Europe has for centuries been used to a paid clergy, though in England, until recently, the money came largely from land owned by the local church, income from which belonged to the vicar or rector so long as he held the 'living'. That is not so far removed from the situation in many a Greek village, where the Orthodox priest is one farmer among others. But in England, the clergy of the national Church were long forbidden to take part in gainful occupations other than farming their own land or taking part in education.

The present interest in self-supporting clergy began with the feeling that a clerical 'caste' could drive a wedge of incomprehension between priest and people. An Anglican missionary priest of very independent mind, Roland Allen, argued early this century that instead of having priests sent to it from outside, a local Christian community should select one of its number and put him up to the bishop for ordination. Such a practice would solve several of the problems of small and scattered local churches in countries such as India.

The experience of French priests ministering in the camps of the Third Reich brought home to them the degree of alienation between the Catholic priest trained in the closed atmosphere of the diocesan seminary and the ordinary Frenchman whom they had previously only met on ceremonial and privileged occasions, if at all. The priest-worker movement applied the wartime lessons to the post-war situation. The subsequent difficulties give food for thought but not necessarily for discouragement.

The English situation is different from the French in that here the Labour movement was not so anti-Christian in its origins. Our own pioneers of industrial mission have tended therefore to prefer the system of industrial chaplains, that is, professional clergy paid by the Church, accepted by both sides of local industry but sponsored by neither or by both. There are, however, some Anglican priests earning their living in ordinary industrial jobs, and a good many others working as teachers, doctors, journalists, policemen, social workers, and doubtless in many other occupations.

The middle Sixties saw an increase of interest in a non-stipendiary ministry. To some extent it was due to a failure of nerve when clergy, unsure of their role in a rapidly changing world, tried to assimilate their ministry to social work, to the lower levels of psychiatric care, to industrial welfare, or to community development. One of the great merits in the essay of Professor Dunstan mentioned in my last letter was the insistence on the distinctive professionalism of the priest. The non-stipendiary priest working in another profession will have two characters to sustain, not a single one modified by another.

The inflationary Seventies seem likely to add their own urgency to the movement for a non-stipendiary ministry. Is it cheating to see here a case of God's will being made plain through economic necessity?

Yours ever,
Gregory

28

15   CONCERNING THE SAME

My dear Christopher,

I think that you are wrong to regard non-stipendiary priesthood as a soft option. Yet many parish clergy undoubtedly do, particularly when they reflect that their part-time curates may be earning four times as much as they are. The proper ways of selecting and training such men, too, are in their infancy, and the type of ministry itself attracts both the glamour and the suspicion of any novelty.

Remember that the non-stipendiary priest is very likely performing his ministerial duties on top of a demanding job; time for his family, for rest, and for recreation will be hard to find. If his paid occupation is one of the learned professions, he will have to make the necessary adjustments between the two 'characters'. How will his character as a priest affect his relations with colleagues, his superiors as well as his juniors? If he is professionally in a position to influence decision-making for a wide community, at what points must he take care that his priestly concerns do not constitute an improper interest? He will be venturing through many uncharted waters. It will take years for the Church to build up a code of professional conduct, or rather several alternative codes, to guide him through the hazards.

Then there are the relations between the priest in secular employment and the active Christian layman who is his colleague. Supporters of industrial mission chaplaincies have often opposed the introduction of priest-workers on the ground that such persons would be usurping the layman's job; they should be servicing the layman, not acting for him. Also, anyone earning his living within the structures of industry is bound to be involved on one side or the other in an industrial dispute. It is wrong, they say, for a priest to be identified with either side, since his pastoral responsibility must extend to both.

The non-stipendiary priest faces similar problems outside the world of industry. Even within the domestic life of the Church, what, for example, is his position compared with that of the commissioned (lay) Reader?

So you see the problems of the non-stipendiary priest are many and serious; his lot may not be unhappy, but it is certainly not easy. But two facts refuse stubbornly to disappear. The Church of England cannot support anything like the number of paid priests that it needs to maintain the services to which its people feel entitled; and a growing number of men (and women too, but that is another question!) seem to be experiencing a persistent sense of being called to priestly ministry while continuing in their existing employment.

The conjunction of those two facts makes me think that this form of ministry, for all its difficulties, may well have a key part to play in God's plans for the future. I hope therefore that you and others like you, who are wondering whether you may be called to the ministry, will be sure to investigate the non-stipendiary avenue of service.

Yours ever,
Gregory

30

16 TO READ OR NOT TO READ
FOR A DEGREE IN THEOLOGY

My dear Christopher,

No, I don't believe that you should switch your university course to do theology; at least, not until you have reached a stage in that course when you would anyway take on a different subject. Incidentally, I should probably say the same thing if you were an apprentice, or an articled clerk, or well on the way to any other basic professional or technical qualification.

One reason for saying that so firmly is that you are still not certain that in the end the ministry will be for you. There is something in your point that the academic study of theology might help you clear your mind one way or the other (though it might not), but the effects of a sudden change could be too damaging to your intellectual training as a whole. If what you really want is to see if you can 'take' church teaching at a serious level, you could get someone competent to prescribe a course of leisure-time reading.

A second reason for completing your present course of studies, even if the occasion for them is less compelling than it was, is to test your 'stickability'; and that is a quality at least as important in the ministry than in any other calling.

Thirdly, you are more likely to profit from the academic study of theology after you have completed a degree course in another subject. It is always something of an ordeal for a person of firm convictions to submit the ground material of his own deep belief to the rigours of critical analysis; but it is easier to see things in perspective when you have previously mastered the techniques and attitudes needed. Those who advise ordinands do not always appreciate this point sufficiently. The result is that too many people

31

taking a first degree in theology find themselves forced into one of two unhappy positions. Either their faith seems to dissolve as they study it; or they save their faith by segregating it rigidly from their academic studies.

I would indeed carry this matter to the point of querying the advice frequently given to potential ordinands before they go up to a university, that they should preferably study theology. I am not persuaded that a single degree in that subject is the best intellectual preparation for the ministry. It is for some, no doubt; but others would be better advised to bring to the climax of a degree that discipline in which they were engaged in the Sixth Form at school; and then, if they are up to it, read for a second degree in theology or else tackle the subject in a less academic context. But you must discuss it with those of your advisers who know you best; it is essentially a matter for individual advice, not for general policy.

Finally, to revert to your query about changing subjects in mid-course, there is the matter of being equipped as well as possible to earn your living. There is a steady need, it is true, for teachers who can specialize in religious studies and, for the high-fliers, a number of university posts; and in many industrial posts theology is as much (or as little) use as any other arts degree. But don't burn your boats before you have to!

Your rather cautious
Gregory

17 CLERICAL POVERTY

My dear Christopher,

I cannot avoid saying that your rejoinder to my crack
about not burning your boats does more credit to your
heart than to your head. Since you asked me once to say
exactly what I think about your attempts to clear your
mind, I shall do so almost brutally. Your reaction was
based on two assumptions, one of them questionable and
the other false.

The questionable one is that if you do turn out to be
called to the priesthood, you should exercise that ministry
through employment as a clergyman. I have already written
about looking at the non-stipendiary alternative. Only if
you are pretty sure your calling is to serve full-time in a
parish, should you rule out the need to make sure you can
earn your living.

The false assumption is that it is suitable, if not actually
desirable, for a priest to be uncomfortably poor. That is
indeed widely believed today; and it is fashionable to
deplore the fact that, at some periods of history, their lot
placed the clergy in a seemingly enviable walk of life. You
often hear it said that our Lord had no visible means of
support but was dependent upon the charity of the good-
hearted. More generally, appeal is made to a spirit of
sacrifice deemed appropriate by way of response to the
sacrifice which our Lord made for us. In addition, hints are
sometimes heard that the clergy, in common with other
'helping' professions, obtain through the performance of
their duties rewards which are greater than mere monetary
satisfaction. It is not always noticed that the last two points
cancel each other out.

If you think about it, you will see that at several points
there is no parallel between the Lord and clergymen of the

Church of England. Matters of high theology apart, clergymen are not expected to exercise their ministry for a maximum of three years only, nor to forswear marriage and family life. On the contrary, most parishioners prefer their clergy to be family men.

The parallel with St Paul, if one wants a precedent from the early Church, is a good deal closer. He insisted on the right of those who served the spiritual needs of the congregation to receive from that congregation enough for their physical needs, and it is not likely that he meant the payment to be niggardly. St Paul was indeed proud to waive his own right to such payment, but he made it quite clear that it was a right, and that his decision not to claim it was his own pleasure and did not commit his colleagues.

Those clergymen, therefore, who rejoice that nowadays economic developments have brought the clergy as a profession to the threshold of poverty, may be proud to exercise their option and waive their rights, but they should not assume that the calling to ministry is necessarily one to poverty. Nor should the layman make the comfortable assumption that the 'sacrifice' properly included in a worthy response to Christ's sacrifice must be one of material poverty.

For sacrifice there must be. I suggest that for our own time that sacrifice is bound to include the elements of irrelevance, availability, and responsibility.

Yours ever,
Gregory

34

18 THE PROPER SACRIFICE
   REQUIRED OF A PRIEST

My dear Christopher,

You ask why I chose those three words, responsibility, availability, and irrelevance, to characterize the true sacrifice which everyone who would be an ordained priest must expect to make. I could, of course, have chosen others, but between them those three cover a great deal of the matter.

The priest's responsibility in spiritual matters is almost endless; at least, it does not end until those for whom he has responsibility have found their eternal destiny, however you interpret that phrase. Read the Bishop's Charge to the candidates presented to him at an ordination. A doctor has fearful responsibility for the life of his patient, but the priest's does not end with the parishioner's death. Moreover his responsibility is not limited to a particular field of concern. It is for the whole person. The sacrifice here is bound to include that of peace of mind.

The availability properly expected of a priest (for there are improper expectations) stems from his responsibility. If people need him for their eternal well-being, he must be there in their hour of need. Most clergy feel obliged to keep open house as far as they can. The consequent sacrifice of time and privacy affects their home and family. Moreover, the priest and his household are constantly under inspection and subject to criticism. They are 'public' and 'professional' Christians and the resultant sacrifices can be hard to bear.

The element of irrelevance is typically today's addition to the sacrifice of the priesthood. Many of the older clergy are bewildered because so much of the work for which they were appreciated thirty years ago has been taken over by the Welfare State. They are less likely than before to be asked to help as a matter of course in matters benefiting the neighbourhood generally. Although there are many hospitals, for example, where the chaplain, often the local vicar, is accepted as a member of the therapeutic team, there are others where his ministrations are considered marginal, perhaps tiresome and even undesirable extras. Even among the people who claim him particularly, time and again the priest will find that even the 'pillars of the Church' in no way share his enthusiasm; that indeed is one of the hardest parts to bear.

It would be false to paint too gloomy a picture, but the undoubted joys of the ministry can be appreciated best against the background of its sorrows. The message is plain. If a priest is to operate efficiently from the base of a normal family life, he must be properly paid. He (and his wife) will need labour-saving equipment, facilities for outside interests and hobbies, decent holidays, freedom from material worries both now and looking ahead to retirement.

All that is far from the case at the moment and inflation continually makes it worse. The only solution is for a great deal of new money to be found quickly. It is the old cliché of the cake. If the laity cannot make the cake a whole lot bigger, there must be fewer clerical mouths to eat it.

You can see why I insist on such a rigorous scrutiny before you commit yourself to full-time ministry. It is in the interest of the Church as well as in your own to be able to support yourself if necessary. If you cannot, I do not think that you should consider ordination or be considered for it.

Yours ever,
Gregory

My dear Christopher,

I shall not come back at you again. I am satisfied that you have faced the issues and have made a fair decision. There is undoubtedly a level where you take note of the 'prudential' issues and decide to go against them. I am delighted that you should express yourself as you do. But — and here I am going to insist — it is only you who have the right to express yourself in that way, and that only in so far as it involves you yourself personally. If there were any question of marriage, for example, you would have to review it all again.

You speak of 'the logic of personal surrender'. You say you 'have been gripped by the love of God as it has come to me in Christ', that you find yourself on a plane of living where the basic dynamic is to respond, to give yourself in gratitude. That sounds authentic, because it is so personal. You say that you are worried because you cannot find the right words in which to express it. That again sounds authentic; for though the experience is widespread among committed Christians, its details vary from one person to another and part of it remains strictly incommunicable.

'The privileges of a servant may include a change in my style of living', you write. Indeed they may. That remark shows the proper flexibility in a genuine sense of call. The other things that you say make it plain that the changes you have in mind are in the direction which conventional standards would call downward. But don't forget that being flexible means that you can bend in more than one direction. Christian propaganda has very properly concentrated on the plight of those in obvious need and poverty, but the others need care too: the minority, the élite, the wealthy. True 'suppleness of spirit' will make it possible for you to be 'kicked upstairs', should that prove to be God's will for you. Beware of false romanticism in assuming a call to the poorest but if, after testing, you still feel drawn to such work, then jump to it gladly.

The question of true surrender is notoriously hard to assess. It is like the matter of the 'call' that we discussed earlier, in that its details will be different for every different person. It is the surrender to God of your personality complete with the background, the limitations, the potentialities, all the factors internal and external which have made you the person you are; and the mix is not the same for any two people.

Here are two practical suggestions for testing it; they are hints only, for this is no area for hard and fast procedures. First, give yourself a periodic check to detect any hang-ups in surrender. Run through the possibilities open to you and look with special care at any you find unwelcome; there may be valid reasons for your negative reaction, but there may not. (Don't, of course, ignore the wishes of anyone who happens to be dependent on you, or the consequences for such a person.) The second hint is to talk over the possibilities with someone who knows you and whose opinion you have cause to respect, before you commit yourself finally one way or the other. Don't feel bound to accept his opinion, and don't back out of your own responsibility for decision; but if you do decide to go against such advice, make sure you accept your own reasons for doing so.

> Yours ever,
> *Gregory*

My dear Christopher,

I thought that the subject of clergymen's wives would come up sooner or later! If the place of the priest in contemporary life is uncertain, how much more that of his wife. Partly it is due to the contemporary woman's dilemma: career or home? A more specific reason is that so much of her husband's work is done from his house or in his house; and in most cases that house is his only because of the appointment he holds. The priest and his wife have indeed a cluster of acute problems which they will have to sort out to their joint satisfaction. Their task is not made easier by the expectations which many parishioners will have. Generalized good advice is pretty futile; the one essential is for each couple to recognize that there are problems, to talk them out and, having decided on a particular style of living, to stick to it unless and until they want to change.

Special problems arise when the husband is ordained in middle life. The wife's adaptation is likely to be harder than her husband's and she will probably get less help. Of course, if she is totally out of sympathy with her husband's vocation, he probably should not be encouraged to go forward, but even the spiritually sympathetic wife of, for example, a bank clerk may not realize how much her husband's presence about the house most mornings may shatter the domestic routine of years. In some cases, there will be a big drop in income to be faced, and the social demands of being the wife of her husband in his new position may not be welcome.

Most theological colleges now have a majority of married students. The advisers of ordinands often feel it better for a man to begin his ministry with his wife beside him rather than to face a second set of adjustments so soon after the crisis of becoming a clergyman. I see the wisdom of it, but I sometimes wonder whether it is not making a virtue out of necessity. Early marriage is generally assumed today to be almost a basic human right in a way it was not a generation ago.

I think that it might well be put to would-be ordinands that they should at least consider whether a proper part of the sacrifice involved in the ministry might not for them be to postpone the joys and the demands of married life for a few years at least. Certainly the Church could do with a 'flying squad' of young priests who could be sent where the need is greatest without having to consider their family responsibilities. At least one group, the Company of Mission Priests, exists to give a framework to such short-term celibacy.

Undoubtedly most lay people who express an opinion on it prefer their parson to be married, but the lady of the vicarage has not always been held in high esteem. Queen Elizabeth I found it hard to tolerate her at all. Half-a-century later George Herbert, whose *A Priest to the Temple* is one of the great formative classics of Anglican writing on ministerial calling, preferred his priest unmarried, on the unfashionable assumption that 'virginity is a higher state than matrimony'.

But one thing must be made plain. If the local church wants to have a family man at the vicarage, it must want it enough to pay for it properly.

Yours ever,
Gregory

My dear Christopher,

I am sure that you are right to be concerned about the cases of disaster among the clergy, but I am equally sure that you should not exaggerate the problem. Considering the total work-force, the number who suffer breakdown, whether physical, mental, or what is sometimes called moral, is very small. The rate of physical breakdown is particularly worrying among the 'top' clergy; recent reorganizations in church administration have tended to overload a small number of over-willing horses and bishops in particular could often be relieved of many chores expected of them. But from the insurance angle, clergy generally are still good risks!

Cases of mental breakdown are, of course, less easily avoided by the application of common sense. When we considered the make-up of the 'pastoral heart', we saw that the good priest was bound to be a vulnerable person; only a sensitive man can help other people deeply. Also, many of the best pastoral clergy are themselves men who have been through some kind of fire. Having themselves struggled to the other side, they can reach out with insight to those who are struggling still, but the fire that they have been through has often marked them.

It is quite artificial to divide people at this level into the strong and the weak. A priest involved in a pastoral relationship often gains from it as much as he gives. But sometimes it drains him dry; sometimes he exposes parts of his character to strains which are stronger than he realizes; sometimes the depression or the degradation with which he is trying to help another person to cope, seems to come across and envelop him too. If the priest is isolated in his ministry, overworked, and perhaps harrassed financially, a breakdown may be the only way of escape open to him. It is no good telling a man to pray more, or reminding him of encouraging texts like 'My grace is sufficient for thee . . .', when what he needs is a month's holiday or a new hot-water system.

You mention those scarifying cases that get into the papers. In fact there are very few of them, though they are always 'news' and so get great publicity. I suppose there are some rogues in every profession, but mostly the cases result from a combination of two things: failure to know one's weak points and guileless zeal unchecked by wiser heads. A parson becomes aware, for example, of prostitution in his parish. He sets out to befriend the girls without realizing that his own marriage has gone a bit stale; and an unscrupulous girl, aided perhaps by her 'protector' and his camera, is quick to take advantage.

Homosexuality gives rise to much the same situation. Most people have some latent homosexual feeling; indeed without some degree of *rapport* it is hard to see how any pastoral relationship could develop. The small number of people for whom their own sex is definitely the more attractive are in most danger where they have not realized it or have tried to ignore it. But the homosexual priest who knows his condition, has accepted it, and embraced it within a rule of chastity will be on his guard against the pitfalls of sudden infatuation. His very condition may be the means through which he is sensitive to other people in their needs. It would be a sad day for the Church if ordination were confined to heterosexuals.

Finally, don't be too much dismayed at the few clerical failures. Marvel, instead, at the great majority who are quietly faithful, often in circumstances which can hardly be called encouraging. Perhaps after all his grace is sufficient.

Yours ever,
Gregory

22. GRACE AND SELF-KNOWLEDGE

My dear Christopher,

I agree with you that ordinands and clergy must be encouraged to know themselves, and that they perhaps need training in self-awareness; but I am not so sure that psychiatric examination should be made a part of regular selection procedures. I think that it is better left available in cases where it seems particularly desirable.

But I like your point taking up my remark about grace. The difficulty in connecting the grace of God with human weakness sometimes springs from the parson's isolation. The need for him to keep confidences may mean that he shoulders an unreasonable load. Sadly, one has to say that sometimes professional pride prevents a man from sharing his difficulties with colleagues from other parishes or with his bishop. 'Parson's Freehold' is meant to give a priest freedom from interference but it can keep him in solitary confinement. The many experiments with 'group ministries' and 'team ministries' have been, in part, attempts to free the clergy from dispiriting isolation, though they sometimes introduce new problems.

Perhaps one may say that the grace of God comes to a man who is open to it in his total situation. It certainly comes to him in his solitariness: when he wrestles in prayer, or meditates on the Word, or simply relaxes in his Father's company. But it can also come in his relationships: at home; with the Parochial Church Council; perhaps in the grind of funeral duties. It can come to him when he is off duty as well as in his official occasions.

There are among others two reasons why dedicated clergy may find the flow of grace trickle and dry up. One is a confusion between the grace of God and our awareness of it. Every clergymen warns people from the pulpit against relying on nice comforting religious feelings; they come and go, their erratic course governed by such mundane factors as the state of one's digestion. But preaching and practice are not always one, and many a tired clergyman forgets that the glow of enthusiasm he sometimes feels is at most a by-product of grace; it is certainly not what grace really is about.

This brings us to the second reason why people 'miss out' on grace: because they think it is a sort of spiritual stuff that you can store up, like petrol in the tank of a car. They miss it, in fact, because their expectation is wrong. They are looking for the wrong thing in the wrong place and so they fail to recognize the real thing when it comes.

God's grace is a name for his goodness, his favour, his smile of approval, if you like. It comes unsolicited, unexpected, undeserved. It is on offer for us to accept at any time, but it always comes fresh; try to hoard it against a rainy day and it vanishes. God has indeed provided certain 'moments' when we may be assured beyond doubt of his grace: supremely the historic 'moment' of the life and death and resurrection of Jesus when God established grace as his definitive way of dealing with mankind. From that supreme 'moment' the different church 'moments' of baptism, Holy Communion, absolution, and blessing all derive their force.

A priest with all the pressures upon him needs a discipline of reminding himself. The regular moments of grace in his faithful use of the sacraments will strengthen his efficiency to receive grace at any and every moment. A split second's reflection in a crisis, 'God is here', and the situation is graced, even in disaster.

Yours ever,
Gregory

23 TO THE SELECTION CONFERENCE

My dear Christopher,

So you and the diocese between you have decided the time is ripe for you to attend an ACCM Selection Conference. I am delighted to hear it.

I'm not at all worried that you still aren't certain whether or not it is right for you to go forward on the path towards ordination right away. You have certainly thought about it enough for the opinion of a panel of competent strangers to be valuable. Also, as you say, you do need specific advice over which options to take in the final year of your university course.

It is more likely than not that you will find the Selection Conference a pleasant as well as helpful experience. Unless you are very unfortunate, the selectors will be human and understanding people, and it will be valuable for you to meet a varied group of possible candidates from any part of the country.

I shall look forward with real eagerness to hear how it all goes, and I shall certainly be thinking of you. God bless you and give you light especially at this testing time.

Yours ever,
Gregory